The 'Parents' Time Off' Series

KIDS' COOKING ACTIVITIES

Cecilia Egan

Illustrations by
Cecilia Egan and Peter Petrovic.

LEAVES of GOLD PRESS

First published in 1996 by Pancake Press
as Kids' Cooking

Revised and updated 2015
Copyright © Leaves of Gold Press 2015
The right of Cecilia Egan to be identified as author of this work has been
asserted in accordance with the Copyright, Designs and Patents Act, 1988.

National Library of Australia Cataloguing-in-Publication entry

Creator: Egan, Cecilia, author.

Title: Kids' cooking activities / Cecilia Egan ;
Elizabeth Alger, illustrator.

Edition: 2nd edition

ISBN: 9781925110708 (paperback)

Series: Parents' time off series ; 3.

Target Audience: For primary school age (6-12 year olds)

Subjects: Cooking--Juvenile literature.

Other Creators/Contributors: Alger, Elizabeth, illustrator.

Dewey Number: 641.5123

LEAVES of GOLD PRESS

ABN 67 099 575 078

PO Box 9113, Brighton, 3186, Victoria, Australia
www.leavesofgoldpress.com

CONTENTS

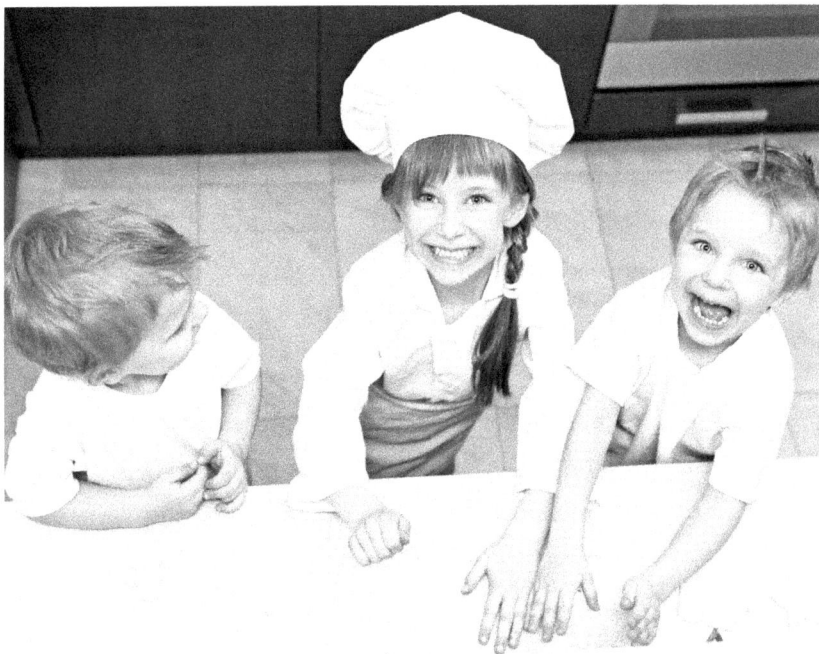

INTRODUCTION

This is a book for children of all ages. The recipes are fun and delicious, and range from the very simple to the more advanced.

Younger children, even those of pre-school age, can use a blunt, broad-bladed knife for spreading sandwiches; an activity they usually love. With a little help from grown-ups, they can even mix and pour the "no-bake" recipes.

Primary school children who can use a sharp knife safely can cut up fruit and vegetables to make the interesting and healthful salads.

Older children, teenagers and beyond, will enjoy using the stove or electric mixer to make the rest of the recipes in this book.

Kid's cookery, in addition to being an absorbing and educational activity, can also be rewarding for the rest of the family when the food is ready to be eaten!

DEDICATION

Dedicated to Jacinta, my four-year-old helper whose enthusiasm is always an inspiration.

CODES USED IN THIS BOOK

The number of stars indicate how easy or difficult the recipe is:

* Very simple.

** Average.

*** More advanced.

(No heat) Indicates that a stove or oven are not used at all.

(No bake) Indicates that only a very *small* part of the recipe requires some cooking.

OVEN TEMPERATURE GUIDE.

Setting	Gas		Electric	
	°F	°C	°F	°C
Low or cool	200	100	200	100
Very Slow	250	120	250	120
Slow or warm	300	150	300-325	150-160
Mod slow	325	160	325-350	160-180
Moderate	350	180	350-375	180-190
Mod hot	375	190	375-400	190-200
Hot	400	200	400-450	200-230
Very hot	450	230	450-500	230-260

WEIGHTS AND MEASURES

Australian Standard Metric measures are used in this book. All cup and spoon measurements are level. As many stoves still in use have fahrenheit temperature gauges, gas oven temperatures have been given in both celsius and fahrenheit.

For temperatures in electric ovens, use the above guide.

RULES OF THE KITCHEN — read these before you start!

Safety Rules:
1. Never touch the hot part of the stove or hot cooking utensils. Use oven mitts on your hands when taking trays out of the oven.
2. If food or liquid is spilt on the floor, clean it up straight away or you might slip on it.
3. Handle knives and other sharp equipment carefully.
4. When a saucepan is on the stove, turn its handle to the side of the stove, so that someone will not accidentally brush against the handle.

General Rules:
1. First, read the recipe carefully.
2. Before starting, collect all your ingredients and the equipment you will need.
3. Weigh and measure ingredients accurately.
4. After cooking, clean up and wash the dishes!

SANDWICHES

SANDWICHES

Sandwiches tast best when they are made with very fresh bread. You can use white or wholemeal slices, bread rolls or pocket bread — (pita bread). If you can't get fresh bread, toast the sandwich, either under the griller or in a jaffle iron. Hot cheese jaffles are especially nice on a cold evening!

Sliced bread sandwiches can be cut in interesting ways —

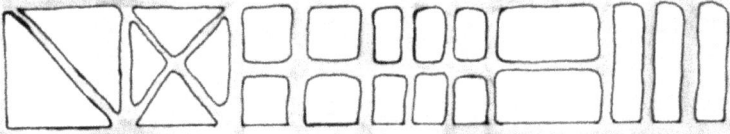

or for parties you can make pinwheel or ribbon sandwiches.

How To Make Sandwiches

Use soft butter or margarine — spread butter thinly on two slices of bread then spread filling on one slice. Put the other slice on top and press firmly down before cutting into suitable shapes.

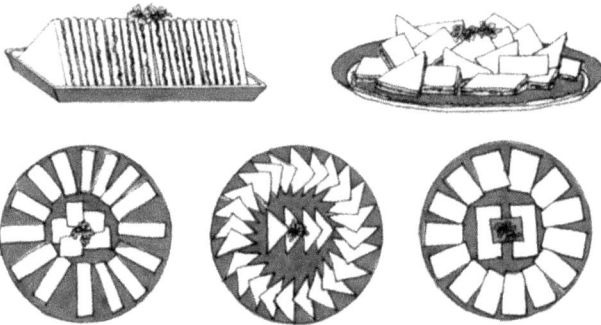

Sandwich Fillings

Here are some suggestions — or you can make up your own.

(a) Vegetable fillings: *lettuce, tomato, asparagus, chopped celery.*

(b) Meat fillings: *slices of chicken, ham, tongue, corned beef or other cold meats.*

(c) Cheese fillings: *sliced or grated cheese.*

(d) Fish fillings: *canned sardine, salmon, tuna.*

(e) Egg fillings: *hard-boiled, chopped egg or cold scrambled egg.*

(f) Prepared fillings: *Vegemite, Promite, peanut butter, lemon butter; cream cheese spead.*

(g) Fruit and Nut fillings: *chopped almonds, walnuts, peanuts, raisins, dates, figs, apple, mashed banana.*

(h) Combination fillings:
peanut butter and mashed banana
cheese slices and tomato
cold sliced sausages with tomato sauce
cream cheese and alfalfa sprouts
chopped walnuts and Vegemite
boiled egg mashed with cream cheese
grated apple and grated cheese
raisins, honey and mashed banana
salmon with mayonnaise and mashed hard-boiled egg
peanut butter with grated carrot

cottage cheese mashed with hard-boiled egg
baked beans with bacon
grated apple, nuts and honey
fish paste with hard-boiled egg
boiled egg and lettuce
liverwurst with sweet corn
lettuce, tomato and asparagus
peanut putter and honey
peanut butter and chopped raisins
cottage cheese with grated apple

PINWHEEL SANDWICHES * (No Heat)

Ingredients:

slices of fresh bread
softened butter or margarine
one or more of the following fillings:
  (each filling will cover
  one slice of bread)
1 tablespoon of cream cheese,
1 tablespoon of fish paste or
  meat paste,
1 tablespoon of canned tuna
  mashed together with mayonnaise,
1 tablespoon of peanut butter.

Equipment:

chopping board
knife for cutting
broad knife for spreading
plastic food wrap
bowls
measuring spoons
plate

Method:

1. Cut the crusts off all the slices of bread and lightly butter each slice.
2. Prepare the fillings you want to use.
3. Spread the fillings on the slices.
4. Roll up each slice of bread separately and wrap in plastic food wrap, making sure the roll won't come undone.
5. Chill the rolls in the refrigerator.
6. After about two hours the rolls should stay rolled up when the plastic wrap is taken off. Remove the wrapping and cut rolls into 1 cm slices.
7. Serve on a plate.

This is 1 cm.

RIBBON SANDWICHES* (No Heat)

Ingredients:
4 slices of fresh bread (2 white
   and 2 brown or all one colour)
2 tablespoons of softened butter
   or margarine
1 piece of slice cheese
1 slice of cold meat eg. ham
sweet green gherkin
spread on thinly sliced tomato.

Equipment:
chopping board
spreading knife
bowls
cutting knife
plate

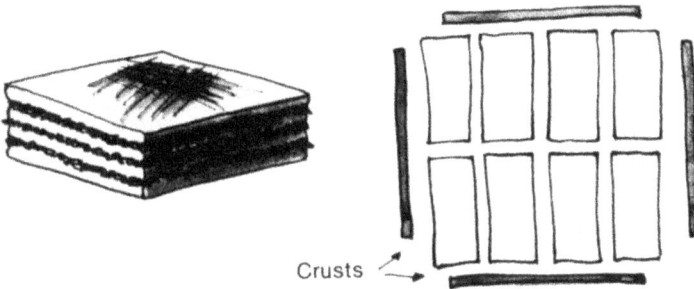

Crusts

Method:
1. Prepare the fillings and soften the butter.
2. Butter two slices of bread (one of each colour, or the same). Put the cheese on one slice and top with the other lice of bread.
3. Butter the top of that sandwich and spread some gherkin on it or place slices of tomato on it.
4. Butter a slice of bread and place over filling.
5. Butter top of sandwich and place the slice of meat on it.
6. Butter the last slice of bread and put it on top of the meat.
7. Cut the crust off and slice into 8 rectangles. Serve on a plate.

PARTY FACE SANDWICHES * (No Heat)

Ingredients:

slices of fresh bread
softened butter or margarine
cream cheese spread or
boiled egg mashed with mayonnaise
or peanut butter or
tuna mashed with mayonnaise
grated carrot (hair)
cheese sticks (nose)
thin wedges of tomato (mouth)
raisins (eyes)
carrot sticks (eyebrows)

Equipment:

chopping board
spreading knife
fork for mashing
bowls
cutting knife
plates

Method:
1. Cut the crusts off the slices.
2. You may leave the slices as rectangles or cut them into a circle shape.
3. Spread with butter or margarine.
4. Spread with either the egg or tuna filling or the cream cheese or peanut butter. (Don't spread too much on!)
5. Now decorate the open sandwich to make faces or designs with the grated carrot, raisins, tomato and cheese sticks.

SALAD ROLL* (No Heat)

Ingredients:

1 roll, long or round, wholemeal
   or white
1 lettuce leaf sliced into long "shreds"
3 slices tomato
2 slices beetroot
2 tablespoons of grated carrot
1 tablespoon of alfalfa sprouts
3 slices of cucumber
soft butter or margarine
1 slice of cheese.

Equipment:

chopping board
cutting knife
spreading knife
grater for carrot
plate
measuring spoons

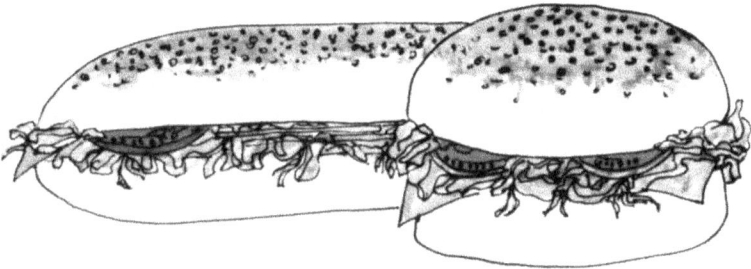

1. Cut the roll in half and butter each side lightly. Prepare the vegetables.
2. Place the salad ingredients on one side of the roll and put the other side on top.
3. Serve on a plate. YUM!

CINNAMON TOAST*

Ingredients:

1 slice hot buttered toast
¼ teaspoon cinnamon
½ teaspoon castor sugar

Equipment:

Chopping board
teaspoon
small bowl
hot serving plate
knife.

Method:

1. Mix cinnamon and sugar and sprinkle over hot buttered toast.
2. Place under hot griller for on minute to melt sugar.
3. Cut into fingers or triangles, and serve on hot serving plate.

CHEESE TOAST*

Ingredients:

1 slice hot buttered toast
1 tablespoon of grated cheese or
*   a slice of cheese*

Equipment:

knife
chopping board
hot serving plate

Method:

1. Place cheese on top of hot buttered toast.
2. Place under hot griller until slightly melted and golden brown.
3. Cut into fingers or triangles and serve on a hot serving plate.

HOT JAFFLES *

Ingredients:

2 slices bread
soft butter or margarine
filling such as
  a slice of cheese
  slices of tomato
  a slice of ham.

Equipment:

chopping board
spreading knife
cutting knife
jaffle iron or
electric jaffle maker.

Method:
1. Butter each slice of bread on *both* sides.
2. Top one slice with cheese or tomato or ham or all three together.
3. Place the other slice on top.
4. Put the sandwich in the jaffle iron or jaffle maker and cook until golden brown.
5. Remove jaffle carefully so as not to burn your fingers (a spreading knife or spatula will help ease it out), cut it in half and eat hot.

SALADS.

SALAD PERSON *** (No Heat)

This salad person can be made for a party or just for fun. Make him or her lying down — it won't stand up — and use thick toothpicks to fix the vegetables together, like this:

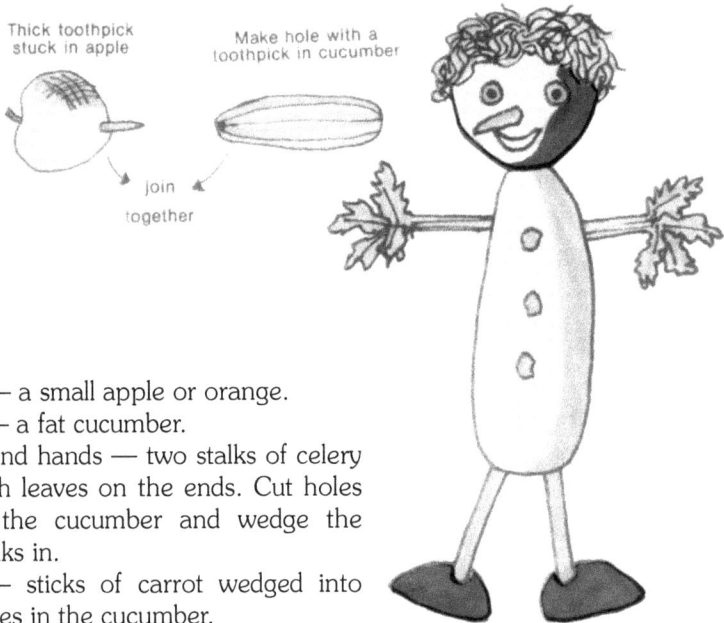

Thick toothpick stuck in apple

Make hole with a toothpick in cucumber

join

together

Head — a small apple or orange.

Body — a fat cucumber.

Arms and hands — two stalks of celery with leaves on the ends. Cut holes in the cucumber and wedge the stalks in.

Legs — sticks of carrot wedged into holes in the cucumber.

Shoes — two radishes with one side cut flat for the soles. Cut holes in radishes and wedge legs in.

Hair — spread mayonnaise on top of the head and cover with grated carrot or grated cheese or bean sprouts.

Eyes and buttons — halved stuffed olives, or raisins, stuck on with toothpicks through the middle.

Mouth — carve a mouth into the skin of the apple or orange.

Nose — a stick of carrot, wedged into a hole you have cut in the apple.

SALAD GARDEN** (No Heat)

A salad garden is made of celery curls and spring onion curls for trees, and radish flowers and tomato flowers. Hard boiled egg flowers can also be used. The "trees" can be fixed upright in cold mashed potato, which can then be covered in shredded lettuce for grass.

Ingredients:

Celery stalks
Spring onions
Firm tomatoes
Radishes
Hardboiled eggs
Cold mashed potato
Shredded lettuce for "grass"

Equipment:

Small cutting knife
Chopping board
Bowl of very cold water
with ice cubes in it
Large plate for arranging garden.

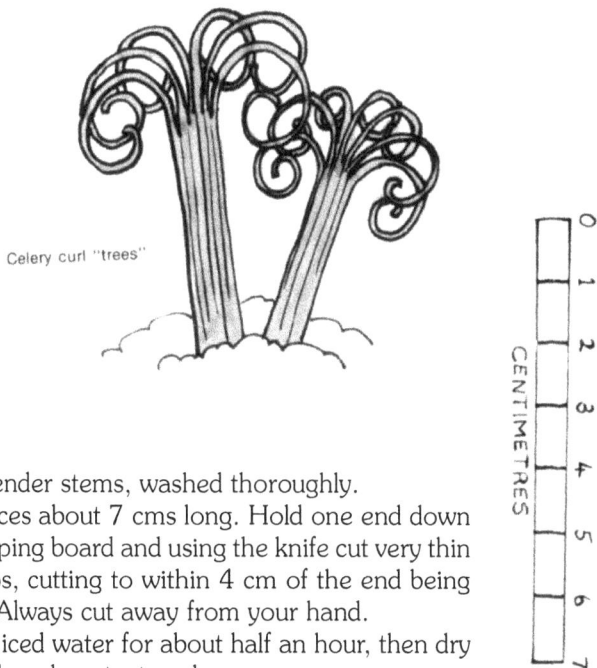

Celery curl "trees"

Celery curls:

1. Use crisp, tender stems, washed thoroughly.
2. Cut into pieces about 7 cms long. Hold one end down on the chopping board and using the knife cut very thin parallel strips, cutting to within 4 cm of the end being held down. Always cut away from your hand.
3. Place in the iced water for about half an hour, then dry carefully with a clean teatowel.

SALAD GARDEN — continued

Spring onion curls**

1. Use about 7 cm at the root end of the onion.
2. Wash onion carefully and cut off roots and any papery outside skin.
3. Place onion on chopping board, grip root end, and with the knife cut lengthwise to within 4 cm of the root end. (Always cut in a direction away from your hand). Repeat this, so that the stem of the onion is cut in four.
4. Place in iced water to curl, then dry carefully with a clean teatowel.

Radish "flowers"

Spring onion
curl "trees"

Radish flowers*:

1. Trim off green leaves, wash radish carefully and scrape off any discoloured part.
2. Hold radish stem down on chopping board and with the knife cut the radish in half from *the root end* down to within 1 cm of the *stem end*. Repeat this once again, so that the radish is almost cut in four sections. If possible, it may be cut in eight sections.
3. Place in iced water for about ½ an hour, for petals to open, then dry with a teatowel.

SALAD GARDEN — continued

Tomato or hard boiled egg flowers**

1. Use a firm tomato, or a hard boiled egg with the shell peeled off, and a small sharp knife.
2. Hold tomato (or egg) in one hand and pierce it with the knife, pushing the knife halfway through the tomato then taking it out, as shown.

(It doesn't matter; if you cut a bit past the halfway mark.)

3. Keep making these deep diagonal cuts to form a zigzag pattern around the "waist" of the tomato or egg.

Make sure all the cuts join at the corners.

4. Pull the egg or tomato apart into two halves, which are the two flowers.
   The centre of the flowers may be decorated with half a red or yellow pickled onion. You can also make these flowers with oranges!

Arrange your salad garden on a plate. You could add a jelly baby and a lolly snake for dessert!

SALAD BOAT * (No Heat)

Ingredients:

3 tablespoons of cold mashed potato
One large lettuce leaf
One thin carrot
two cooked prawns or
Two baby carrots
Thinly shredded lettuce

Equipment:

Small plate
Chopping board
Cutting knife
Vegetable peeler

Method:

1. Heap the mashed potato in the middle of the plate.
2. Peel the carrot and fix it upright in the potato for the boat's mast.
3. With the knife poke two holes in the lettuce leaf sail; one near the top and one near the bottom, and put these holes over the carrot to fix the sail to the mast.
4. The prawns or baby carrots are the people in the boat. Fix them into the potato and spread shredded lettuce around for the sea.

CANDLE FRUIT SALAD * (No Heat) For Two People

Ingredients:

Two rings of canned pineapple
One banana
Two cherries — fresh, canned or glacé
Four lettuce leaves

Equipment:

Two plates
Chopping board
Knife

Method:

1. Lay two pieces of lettuce on each plate so that the frilly edges make a nice border around the plates.
2. Lay a slice of pineapple on the lettuce.
3. Cut the banana in half, across.
4. Stand a half banana in the middle of each pineapple ring.
5. Put a cherry on the top of each banana "candle" for a flame. Press it on lightly.

Note: If you aren't going to eat this fruit salad straight away, squeeze lemon juice over the banana. Lemon juice stops peeled banana and apple from going brown.

CANTELOUPE BOATS* (No Heat)

Ingredients:

1 wedge of canteloupe (or rockmelon)
2 tablespoons of fruit yoghurt ½ cup of seedless grapes

Equipment:

Spreading knife
Measuring spoons and cups
Bowl

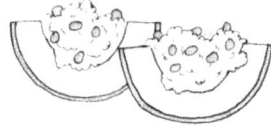

Method:
1. Scoop the seeds out of the canteloupe.
2. Put the wedge of canteloupe in the bowl.
3. Spread yoghurt on canteloupe and decorate with grapes.
4. Chill in the refrigerator before serving.

PINEAPPLE BASKET*** (No Heat).

Ingredients:

One whole pineapple
*Any other fruits such as apple, orange, banana, straw-
    berries, kiwi fruit, grapes, watermelon, canteloupe,
    peaches, raspberries*
Fruit juice

Equipment:

Knife
Chopping board
Spoon

Method:
1. Cut the top ⅓ off the pineapple and scoop out the pineapple flesh with the knife and spoon leaving the skin whole.
2. This makes a container, into which you can put all the other fruits, chopped up and mixed together with fruit juice!
3. Put the top back on for a lid.

SAVOURY SNACKS

SAVOURY TULIPS*

Ingredients:

12 slices fresh bread
½ cup softened butter
1 cup savoury filling, (such as finely
   chopped chicken, salmon, canned
   sweet corn, bacon) mixed with
   white sauce or by itself.

Equipment:

Metal patty trays. (deep)
Measuring cups.
Spreading knife.
Cutting knife.
Serving plate.
Spoon

Method:

1. Cut the crusts off the bread slices and spread with the softened butter.
2. Force bread slices into patty tins, buttered side down. The sticking-up corners form the tulip petals:
3. Bake in a moderate oven 180°C (350°F) gas for 15 minutes, until lightly coloured golden brown.
4. Remove from oven, allow to cool, then fill with the savoury filling.
5. Serve either cold or reheated.

WHITE SAUCE FOR FILLING***

Ingredients:

1 tablespoon butter
2 tablespoons sifted plain flour
1 cup milk

Equipment:

small saucepan ("non-stick" if possible) stirring spoon.

Method:

1. Melt the butter in the saucepan then take the saucepan off the heat.
2. Add the flour and stir until smooth.
3. Return saucepan to a gentle heat and cook for one minute, stirring all the time.
4. Take the saucepan off the heat again, add milk, stir until smooth.
5. Return to heat, stir until boiling. Boil two or three minutes.

DAMPER***

This is the traditional food of the Australian swagman, and used to be cooked in the hot ashes of the campfire. However it will taste almost as good from your oven!

Damper also used to be made only from flour, water and salt, and eaten with a mug of black tea; eggs and milk couldn't be carried around in the swagman's pack under the hot sun!

In the comfort of our homes we can make Damper a little differently.

Ingredients:

3 level cups of self-raising flour
¾ teaspoon of salt
30g of butter or margarine.
½ cup of water
½ cup milk
1 egg (beaten)

Equipment:

Bowl
Flour sifter
Knife
Greased oven tray
Floured board
Pastry brush

Method:

1. Preheat oven to 220°C (425°F) gas or electric.
2. Sift flour and salt into a bowl, chop the butter into the bowl and rub the butter into the flour and salt mixture with your fingertips until the mixture looks like breadcrumbs.
3. Mix the water and milk together.
4. Make a well in the centre of the dry ingredients, add the combined water and milk all at once, mix lightly with a knife, in a cutting motion, until a soft dough is formed.
5. If the dough is too wet, add more flour.

6. Put the dough onto a board lightly sprinkled with flour and knead it lightly.
7. Shape the dough into a ball and put it onto the oven tray, which you have greased with butter.
8. Pat the dough out to a 15 cm (6 inch) circle. With a sharp knife, cut two slits across the dough, about 1 cm (½ inch) deep, like this.
9. With the pastry brush or your fingers, brush the top of the damper with milk, sift a little extra flour over.
10. Bake in a hot oven 200°C (400°F) gas for 10 minutes or until golden brown. Reduce heat to moderate 180°C (350°F) gas, cook a further fifteen minutes, until the damper sounds "hollow" when you gently tap it.

Yummy Damper Variations:

A. You can shape your damper any way you like, eg. plaiting it, twisting it into a circle or making a boomerang shape.
B. Instead of milk, brush the top with beaten egg and sprinkle on poppy seeds or sesame seeds.
C. Add to your damper mixture (before you add the liquid) 30g chopped nuts and 60g chopped dried fruits eg. figs, dates, raisins or sultanas.

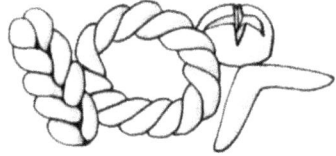

Damper is nicest eaten hot!

CHEESE SAVOURIES*

Ingredients:

1 cup grated cheese
1 small egg (raw)
2 rashers bacon
¼ teaspoon mustard (if you like).
4 slices of bread
Softened butter or margarine

Equipment:

Measuring cup
Grater
Cutting knife
Spreading knife
Oven tray
Bowl
Serving plates.

Method:

1 Mix together the cheese, egg and mustard in the bowl.
2. Butter the bread slices, spread the cheese mixture thickly on top.
3. Cut each slice into four long "fingers", and put the fingers on the baking tray.
4. Chop the bacon into very small pieces and sprinkle on the savouries
5. Bake in a hot oven 200°C (400°F) gas and serve immediately.

POTATOES IN THE FIRE *

Cook these in the hot embers of your campfire, home fireplace or barbecue. Push them deep amongst the glowing coals and cover them with coals. Don't put them into the flames or they will cook too fast on the outside. Use long barbecue tongs and be careful not to burn yourself!

Ingredients:

Large potatoes
Butter or margarine
Grated cheese (if you like)

Equipment:

Aluminium foil
Knife
Long barbecue tongs
Serving plate
Spoon.

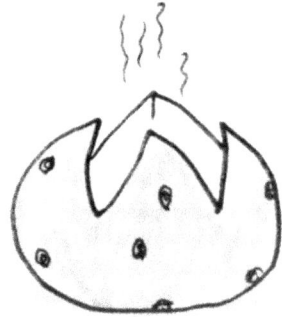

Method:

1. Scrub any dirt off the potatoes but do not peel them. They should be baked "in their jackets". Cut out any spots or marks that don't look good to eat.
2. Wrap each potato well, in aluminium foil. Make sure they're tightly wrapped.
3. Place in the hot embers of the fire as described above. Let them bake for about 2 hours until, when pricked with a skewer, they feel soft right throught to the middle.
4. Remove from fire, place on plate and peel off foil.
5. Make two deep cuts in a cross shape and fill with butter, cheese or both.
6. The skin will probably be blackened so scoop the hot baked potato out of its skin with a spoon to eat it!

EGG AND BACON PIE**

Ingredients:

Two sheets of ready-rolled shortcrust pastry.
6 rashers of bacon
6 eggs
Chopped parsley
   (if you like)
Pepper.
¼ cup of milk
Butter

Equipment:

Deep pie plate
Cutting knife
Measuring cup
Fork

Method:

1. Rub some butter all over the pie plate or grease it so that the pie won't stick.
2. Line the pie plate with one pastry sheet, cutting off the corners that stick out and using them to fill gaps.
3. Trim the rind off the bacon and chop it into medium-sized pieces, place pieces on the pastry base.
4. Break the eggs over the bacon, sprinkle with pepper and chopped parsley.
5. With a pastry brush or your fingers, brush water around the edge of the piedish so that the top layer of pastry will stick.
6. Cover with the other pastry sheet and pinch the edges into a frill or mark edges with a fork.
7. Brush the milk over the top of the pie (this makes it turn brown) and prick the top all over with the fork.
8. Bake for 10 minutes in a hot oven 200°C (400°F) gas then turn the oven down to moderate 180°C (350°F) gas for 20 to 25 minutes. Remove from oven and serve.

BUTTERED POPCORN*

Ingredients:

½ cup unpopped "popping corn"
2 tablespoons oil
Butter
Salt

Savoury Snacks

Equipment:

Large saucepan with lid or electric
trypan with glass lid.
Bowl.

Method:

1. Heat oil in saucepan until very hot.
2. Add corn, put lid on saucepan, shake over the heat until the popping
   sound stops.
3. Place popped corn into a bowl, dot with butter and sprinkle with salt.

SAVOURY ROUNDS**

Ingredients:

2 eggs (lightly beaten)
Some chopped bacon pieces
1 packet of potato chips (crush
   with fork as you go.)
½ chopped up green pepper
¼ teaspoon mixed herbs
2 sheets of ready-rolled puff pastry.

Equipment:

Fork
Knife
Chopping board
Bowl
Greased baking tray

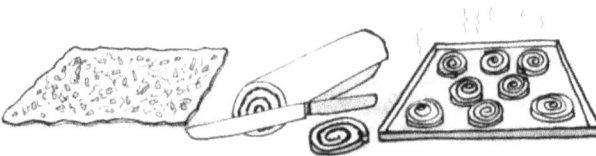

Method:
1. Mix together everything except pastry.
2. Spread mixture over pastry sheets, roll into logs and put into freezer— as it is then easier to cut into ½ cm. slices.
3. Lay the slices on the greased tray and bake in a moderate oven 180°C (350°F) gas for 15 to 20 minutes. Serve hot!

HAMBURGERS **

Ingredients:

1½ kilograms minced steak
1 teaspoon nutmeg
¼ cup chopped parsley
1 cup chopped bacon
1 egg
½ onion finely chopped
½ cup breadcrumbs
¼ teaspoon pepper
Butter for frying.

Equipment:

Knife
Bowl
Spoon
Electric food processor
(of you have one)
Frypan
Egg-lifter

Method:
1. Mix everything together, blending well. An electric food processor makes this very easy.
2. With your fingers press the mixture tightly into flat hamburger shapes.
3. Melt the butter in the frypan and fry the hamburgers until cooked; about 5 minutes on each side.
4. Serve in a buttered roll with lettuce and tomato.

FRENCH TOAST*

French Toast can be a savoury or sweet snack, depending on what you top it with. For a sweet snack, top with jam, lemon juice and sugar, or maple syrup. For a savoury snack use grated cheese or a prepared meat paste, or just eat it by itself.

Ingredients:

2 eggs
½ cup milk
Sliced white bread
Butter or margarine.

Equipment:

Wide bowl Fork
Frypan (electric or stovetop)
Metal egglifter or Spatula.
Plate.

Method:

1. Put two walnut-sized lumps of butter into the frypan and heat frypan until butter melts. Don't let the butter go brown!
2. With the fork, beat the eggs and milk together in the bowl.
3. Dip each slice of bread into this mixture until both sides of the bread are soaked.
4. Fry the soaked slices of bread in the melted butter on both sides until golden brown.
5. Serve hot, with your favourite topping.

SWEET SNACKS

FRENCH CHEWS * (No Bake)

Ingredients:

½ tin condensed milk
½ cup chopped crystallised ginger OR
½ cup chopped crystallised cherries
½ teaspoon cinnamon
1 cup cornflakes (crushed)
¼ cup sweet biscuit crumbs
   (eg. Marie biscuits)
Butter (for greasing tray)

Equipment:

Mixing bowl
Mixing spoon
Oven tray
Measuring cups
Plastic bags
Rolling pin for crushing.

Method:

1. Crush the biscuits by breaking them into pieces and putting them in a plastic bag then rolling over them with a rolling pin, pressing hard. Crush the cornflakes in the same way.
2. Mix together all the ingredients and place in spoonfuls on the greased tray.
3. Bake in a slow oven 150°C (300°F) gas.

HOME-MADE ICY-POLES * (No Heat)

You will need to use special freezer trays for making "icy-poles", which can be bought at supermarkets. A blender is also useful.
Here are some ideas for delicious icy-poles:

Flavoured milk
½ yoghurt and ½ fruit juice
Mixed fruit juices
Yoghurt blended with banana
½ fruit juice with ½ fruit purge.

Milk with chopped nuts
Milk with shredded coconut
Yoghurt with chopped Dried fruit and honey
½ ice-cream and ½ banana or apricot blended together.
Lemonade.

Note: Chopped nuts are not suitable for children under the age of six years.

FROZEN ORANGES * (No Heat)

Just put some fresh oranges in the freezer overnight until they are frozen through. A cool, sweet snack for a hot summer's day.

TOFFEE APPLES***

Ingredients:

1 cup sugar
1/4 cup water
Pinch of cream of tartar
6 medium-sized apples
¼ teaspoon red food colouring.

Equipment:

Saucepan
Spoon
6 strong wooden sticks or skewers
Bowl of cold water
Greased oven tray.

Method:

1. Wash the apples and wipe them completely dry. Push a wooden skewer firmly into each one.
2. Heat sugar, water and cream of tartar in saucepan, stirring until the sugar dissolves and the mixture boils.
3. Boil without stiring until, when a spoonful of the toffee is dropped into cold water, it immediately hardens with a crackling sound. (290°F or 140°C if you have a toffee thermometer.)
4. Remove the toffee from the heat and dip the apples in *quickly* before it has time to set, twisting each one around to coat it well.
5. Stand on a greased tray to set, with sticks upright.

FRUIT SLICE **

Ingredients:

½ cup margarine or butter
1 cup light brown sugar
1 egg
½ cup chopped walnuts
½ cup sultanas
1½ cups Self Raising flour.

Equipment:

Small saucepan
Spoon
Bowl
Greased shallow oven tray
Serving plate with paper doiley.

Method:

1. In the saucepan, mix together the butter and sugar over a low heat until the sugar is dissolved.
2. In the bowl, beat the egg well then add to it the sugar mixture.
3. Mix in the walnuts and sultanas. When it is mixed well, add the flour and mix some more.
4. Grease the oven tray by rubbing it with butter; press the mixture firmly into the tray.
5. Bake for fifteen to twenty minutes in a moderate 180°C (350°F) gas.
6. Allow the slice to cool slightly before cutting it into squares.
7. Put a paper doiley on the serving plate and pile the slices on top.

YUMMY SQUARES* (No Bake)

Ingredients:

125 grams butter
½ cup honey
½ cup milk
½ cup raw peanuts
½ cup coconut
½ cup raisins, (chopped.)
½ cup wheatgerm

Equipment:

Saucepan
Spoon
Blender
Knife
Greased, shallow container.

Method:

1. Chop the peanuts or grind them in a blender.
2. Melt butter and honey over gentle heat in saucepan.
3. Add the remaining ingredients, stir well. If the mixture is too thin, add more chopped fruit or nuts.
4. Pour mixture into greased, shallow container and chill it well in the refrigerator.
5. When it is set, cut it into squares.

* **Note:** recipes containing whole or chopped nuts should not be given to children under 6 years. Nuts should be finely ground.

GINGERBREAD MEN***

Ingredients:

125 g. butter (at room temperature)
125 g. sugar
280 g. flour
½ teaspoon bicarb soda
1½ teaspoons ground ginger
½ teaspoon of cinnamon
½ teaspoon of nutmeg
1 cup warm golden syrup
Currants
Glacé (crystallized) cherries
White icing to decorate. Piping bag.

Equipment:

Bowl
Wooden spoon for creaming OR
Electric mixer for creaming
Wooden board
Small saucepan
Rolling pin
Greased oven tray
Egg-lifter
Wire rack for cooling
Oven mitts.
Piping bag.

Method:

1. Cream the butter and sugar together until very soft. This means you keep mashing them with the wooden spoon or mixer, until they are completely mixed and the mixture looks like cream.
2. Mix in all the other ingredients except the currants, cherries and icing.
3. Warm the golden syrup in the small saucepan until it is runny (not too hot) and mix in enough of it to make a soft dough. You may not need all of it.

4. Knead the dough. Sprinkle the board with some flour and roll the dough out flat on it, with the rolling pin. 1 cm. Make it about ½ cm to 1 cm thick.
5. Cut out man, lady, and baby shapes, with cutters from a shop, or cardboard patterns and a sharp knife. You can use the patterns shown in this book.
6. Put the figures on a greased tray, add currants for eyes and buttons, cherry slice for mouth.
7. Bake in a moderate oven 180°C (350°F) gas for 10 to 15 minutes.
8. Leave the biscuits on the oven tray for a while to cool slightly before lifting them onto a wire rack. (Otherwise they break while being lifted).
9. When cold, decorate (if you like) with white icing from a piping bag.

APRICOT BALLS* (No Heat)

Ingredients:

½ tin condensed milk
250 g. dried apricots
1 cup coconut
Icing sugar.

Equipment:

Blender or chopping knife
Spoon
Bowl
Plate

Method:

1. Mince apricots finely in a blender or food processor, or chop with the knife.
2. Mix with condensed milk and coconut.
3. Form into balls and roll in icing sugar.

CEREAL BALLS* (No Heat)

Ingredients:

1 cup muesli
2 tablespoons wheatgerm
1 tablespoon honey
1 tablespoon peanut butter
¼ cup chopped raisins
Milk
Coconut

Equipment:

Blender
Covered container

Method:

1. Grind muesli and in the blender, add remaining ingredients except milk, and blend.
2. Add as much milk as is needed to bind the mixture together so that you can roll it into balls.
3. Roll in coconut and chill in a covered container in the refrigerator.

FRUIT AND NUT LOAF **

Ingredients:

1 cup All-Bran or other prepared
bran breakfast cereal
1 cup milk
1 cup wheatgerm
½ teaspoon salt
1 teaspoon bicarbonate of soda
1 tablespoon honey
1½ cups mixed dried fruit
½ cup chopped walnuts.

Equipment:

Large mixing bowl
Measuring cups and spoons
Mixing spoon
Two greased loaf tins OR
A greased loaf tin
measuring 23 cm x 13 cm x 8 cm
Wire cooling rack

Method:

1. In the bowl, soak the bran in the milk for five minutes to make it soft.
2. Add all the other ingredients and mix thoroughly.
3. Spoon the mixture into the tins and bake in a moderately hot oven 190°C (375°F) gas —
   in two tins, for 35 to 40 minutes OR
   in one tin, for 45 to 50 minutes.
4. Allow loaves to cool slightly in the tin before turning them out onto a wire rack to cool
5. Slice the loaves and eat them, still warm spread with butter.

QUEEN OF HEARTS' JAM TARTS *

Ingredients:
1 sheet of ready-rolled sweet
  short pastry
Butter
Your favourite jam

Equipment:
Knife
Scone cutter or
Paper circle pattern
Oven patty tins
Chopping board
Teaspoon

Method:
1. Lay the pastry flat on the chopping board and cut out as many circles as you can. If using a paper pattern, make it about 7 cm wide, lay the pattern on the pastry and cut around the edges with a sharp knife.
2. Lightly grease the patty tins with butter and fit a pastry circle into each tin.
3. To decorate the edges press them with a fork or pinch them between your fingers.
4. Place in a moderate oven 180°C (350°F) gas for ten minutes.
5. Remove from oven, put two teaspoons of your favourite jam into each case and return to oven for another five minutes or until pastry is golden brown. Cool before eating!

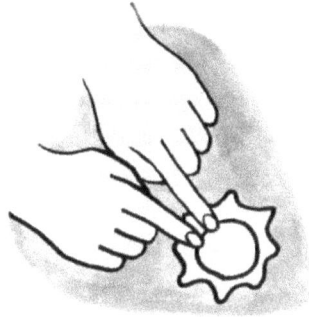

MUESLI MUNCHIES * (No Bake)

Ingredients:

1 cup muesli
1 cup coconut
⅓ cup chopped dried apricots
2 large tablespoons of honey
1½ tablespoons of butter
½ cup boiling water.

Equipment:

Bowl
Mixing spoon
Paper cupcake holders
Knife
Measuring spoons
Tray

Method:

1. In the bowl, mix together the butter, honey and boiling water. Stir until the butter is melted and the honey dissolved. You might have to add a little more hot water.
2. Mix in all the rest of the ingredients, then spoon the mixture into the paper cups and press each one down firmly.
3. Chill the munchies in the fridge on a tray, for two hours.

DESSERTS

BANANAS IN JELLY* (No Bake)

Ingredients:

1 packet jelly crystals
Boiling water
4 bananas

Equipment:

Bowl
Wooden spoon
Measuring cup
Knife
Glass serving bowl

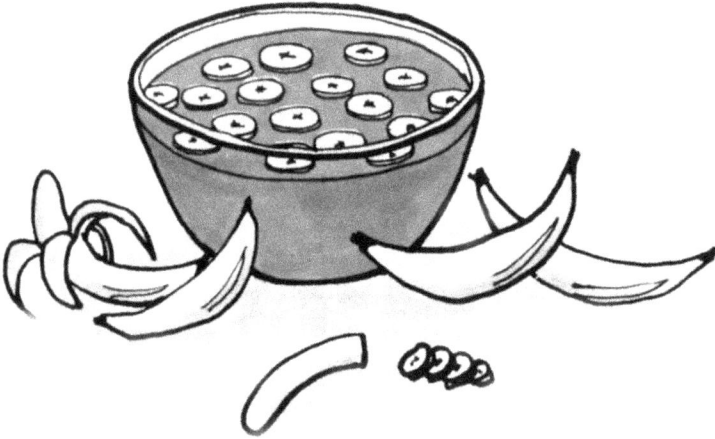

Method:

1. Put the jelly crystals in the basin and add the boiling water, as it says on the packet.
2. Stir until all crystals are dissolved. Allow to cool.
3. Peel and slice the bananas, put them in the glass serving bowl and pour cool jelly over them.
4. Put in the refrigerator until set.

CHOCOLATE BLANC MANGE **

Blanc mange is pronounced "blummondge" and is French for "white food". However chocolate blanc mange is chocolate coloured! It is one of my favourite desserts. For an interesting shape, you can make it in a jelly mould.

Ingredients:

2 tablespoons cornflour
1 tablespoon sugar
4 drops vanilla essence
300ml milk
1 tablespoon cocoa

Equipment:

Bowl
Wooden spoon
Measuring tablespoon
Saucepan (nonstick if possible)
Wetted moulds (if you like)
Or Serving bowl.

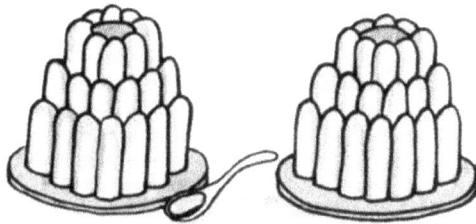

Method:

1. In the bowl, blend cornflour, cocoa and sugar with a little of the milk to make a smooth creamy paste.
2. Heat the rest of the milk in the saucepan until it is almost boiling.
3. Pour hot milk over blended cornflour, cocoa and sugar, *stirring all the time.*
4. Return to saucepan and stir over heat until boiling. Cook for ½ a minute, stirring all the time.
5. Add vanilla essence and pour into the moulds, (which should be wet) or the serving bowl.
6. Refrigerate until cold and set. Serve with cream.
7. To unmould, hold the mould in a bowl of hot water for a short time to loosen the blanc mange, then put a plate on top and turn it upside down. Blanc mange should drop out onto the plate.

Yum!

BREAD AND BUTTER PUDDING. **

Ingredients:
Slices of bread and butter
½ cup sultanas
1 tablespoon sugar
¼ teaspoon vanilla essence
3 pinches of nutmeg
2 cups milk
2 eggs

Equipment:
Casserole dish
Bowl
Fork
Roasting dish

Method:
1. Lay the slices of buttered bread in a buttered casserole dish, sprinkling the sultanas in between the layers but not on top.
2. Beat eggs and sugar with the fork in the bowl and add the milk and essence. Mix well.
3. Pour milk mixture over the bread and butter, sprinkle with nutmeg.
4. Stand the casserole uncovered in the roasting dish filled with warm water, bake in a moderate oven 180°C (350°F) gas, until the milk and egg mixture sets, and is not runny any more.
5. Serve hot!

NOTE: Instead of sultanas, you might like to spread jam thinly on each slice.

PARTY FUN FOODS

CRYSTALLIZED VIOLETS AND ROSE PETALS**

(No Heat)

Ingredients:

flowers or petals
250 g. castor sugar
blue or red food
  colouring
1 teaspoon
  gum arabic   *(available*
2 teaspoons   *at chemists)*
  rose-water

Equipment:

small screwtop bottle
teaspoon, sieve soft
paintbrush saucer,
plate wire rack netting

Method:

1. Dissolve the gum arabic in the rose-water in the small screwtop bottle, shaking the bottle occasionally. Pour this mixture into a saucer or small bowl. To stop the flowers fading, add a drop or two of matching colouring to the mixture.
2. With the soft brush, lightly paint the front and back of each petal or flower, making sure the whole petal/flower is coated.
3. Place each coated petal on the plate which has been covered with a layer of castor sugar.
4. Put castor sugar in the sieve and shake it over the petals.
5. Place petals on a wire rack covered with a piece of coarse netting, to dry in a warm place at a temperature not more than 40°C. You can do this by leaving them in a gas oven heated only by the pilot light for 2 to 4 hours until brittle, turning them every hour so that they dry evenly. Take them out and leave them for about 6 hours to dry completely. Or, simply place them near a radiator to dry for three days.

RABBITS EATING LETTUCE * (No Bake)

Serves 4

Ingredients:

4 canned pear halves
1 pkt green jelly crystals
whipped cream
8 cloves
8 blanched almonds
coconut

Equipment:

beater for whipping cream
bowl for jelly
bowl for cream
large flat serving plate
spoon, knife
measuring cup

Method:

1. Place green jelly crystals in bowl, add boiling water as directed on packet, stir until crystals are dissolved, cool and allow to set in refrigerator. (This could take a few hours.) Chop up jelly.
2. On the large flat serving plate arrange the chopped-up jelly in the centre, for the lettuce.
3. Arrange the four pear halves around the jelly, with the small ends facing in to the centre.
4. Stick two blanched almonds in each of the small ends, for the ears. Put in cloves for eyes.
5. Place a blob of whipped cream against the large end of the pear for the rabbit's tail.
6. Sprinkle coconut between the rabbits. (You can make green coconut for grass by rubbing green food colouring through the coconut.)

MARZIPAN FRUIT * (No Heat)

These tiny, colourful sweets can be piled in a dish for an attractive table decoration, and eaten later! Marzipan is made from almonds and sugar, and can be moulded like clay.

Ingredients:

packet of plain marzipan
(can be bought from supermarkets.)
food colourings
  — red
  — green
  — yellow

Equipment:

small paint brushes
serving dish
small containers for colourings
small bowl of water for
  washing brushes
paper towelling to soak up drips

Method:

1. Take a small piece of marzipan, about the size of a marble or a walnut, and roll it between your palms into a ball.
2. Mix together red and yellow food colouring (a small amount) — add a few drops of water for a paler colour, and paint your orange. Put a tiny green dot on top for the stem!
3. Shape apples, pears, plums, lemons, strawberries and bananas all about the same size. Pineapples are a bit harder to make.
4. Paint apples green or yellow and red, pears yellow and green, bananas and lemons yellow, plums and strawberries red. (If you want purple plums, buy blue food colouring and mix with red.)
5. Put the fruits into a small dish. If you like you can decorate them with lolly "mint leaves".

JELLY ORANGES * (No Bake)

Ingredients:

two large oranges
2 pkts different coloured jellies
boiling water

Equipment:

Citrus juice squeezer
tray
2 bowls teaspoon mixing
spoon measuring cup
serving dish

Method:

1. Cut the oranges in half, crosswise.
2. Use the juicer to squeeze the juice out of each half, then clean the shells out with the teaspoon, being careful not to make any holes in the shells. Drink the juice!
3. Put the different coloured jelly crystals into the bowls and add the boiling water as instructed on the packets. Let the jelly cool to room temperature.
4. Place the shells on the tray, pour one colour jelly into two, and the other colour into the other two.
5. Chill in the refrigerator until set.
6. Just before serving, cut each half into two and arrange the wedges on a serving dish.

CHEESE DIP* (No Heat)

Ingredients:
1 x 125g package of cream cheese
1 packet of French Onion Soup
2 to 3 tablespoons of milk or cream

Equipment:
bowl
wooden spoon
measuring spoons serving bowl

Method:
1. Put the cheese (at room temperature) in the bowl, add the milk and mix together with the wooden spoon until soft.
2. Add the dried soup and mix well.
3. Serve the dip in the bowl, and scoop it out with dry biscuits, carrot sticks or celery sticks.

HAM ROLL-UPS * (No Heat)

Ingredients:

slices of ham
some lettuce
asparagus spears OR
long gherkins sliced lengthwise
OR
cheese sticks OR
bananas sliced lengthwise

Equipment:

chopping board
knife
toothpicks
plate

Method:

1. Place one of the above fillings on each slice of ham, diagonally.
2. Roll it up tightly and stick a toothpick into it to fasten it together.
3. Serve on a plate, on a bed of lettuce.

CELERY BOATS * (No Heat)

Ingredients:

sticks of celery
cream cheese or cottage cheese
paprika

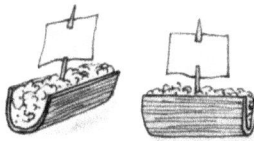

Equipment:

spreading knife
chopping board
cutting knife
plate
toothpicks
paper and scissors

Method:

1. Wash and dry the celery stalks, and fill them with the cheese.
2. Sprinkle with paprika and cut into 5 cm lengths.
3. Cut squares of paper 3 cm x 3 cm. If you like you can use coloured paper, or colour the paper with pencils.
4. Put a toothpick through each square and stick your sails in each boat. Serve on a plate.

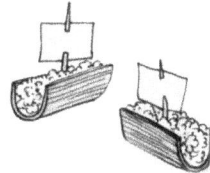

PARTY MICE * (No Heat)

Ingredients:

6 large dessert prunes
12 silver cachous (little sugar-balls)
6 thin strips of licorice
6 toothpicks

Equipment:

knife
plate
chopping board

Method:

1. With your fingers make a small hole in each prune to remove the stone.
2. Cut the licorice into thinner strips if necessary, fix the strips onto the prunes with toothpicks, for tails.
3. Press on silver cachous for eyes.
4. Scatter these little mice in hiding places all over the party table!

SAUSAGE ROLLS**

Ingredients:

250 g frozen prepared short crust pastry
375 g sausage meat
¼ teaspoon salt
some flour for rolling pastry
2 teaspoons chopped parsley
1 small finely chopped onion
some milk

Equipment:

floured board
rolling pin
bowl
mixing spoon
oven tray
serving plate

Method:

1. In the bowl mix the meat with the chopped parsley, onion and salt. Shape into two long rolls.
2. Roll the pastry into a rectangle about 30 cm long by 20 cm wide. Cut it in half lengthwise and trim the edges to straighten them.
3. Place half of meat on each piece of pastry, brush the edges lightly with water to make the pastry stick together, and roll them up.
4. Cut each roll into four and mark the tops by pressing the knife lightly into the pastry in parallel lines.
5. Place on a greased oven tray and brush with milk.
6. Place on the top shelf of a hot oven 200°C (400°F) gas for ten minutes, then reduce heat to moderate 180°C (350°F) for ten to fifteen minutes. Serve hot.

HONEY JUMBLES *

Ingredients:

90 g butter
60 g sugar
1 tablespoon honey
150 g cornflakes

Equipment:

saucepan
wooden spoon
tablespoom
paper cupcake holders
oven tray
wire cooling rack

Method:

1. Place the paper cupcake holders on the tray.
2. Melt butter, sugar and honey together in the saucepan over a low heat, stirring with the wooden spoon.
3. Put the cornflakes in a basin and pour on the warm honey mixture. Mix gently to avoid crushing the cornflakes.
4. Put into the paper holders and cook for 10 minutes in a moderate oven 180°C (350°F) gas.
5. Cool on the wire rack.

FESTIVE RECIPES

WHITE CHRISTMAS * (No Bake)

Ingredients:

1 cup coconut
1 cup powdered milk
1 cup rice bubbles
1 cup icing sugar
1 cup mixed fruit
2 teaspoons vanilla essence
½ cup chopped glacé cherries
250 grams copha.

Equipment:

Spoon
Bowl
Small saucepan
Shallow oventray
Storing jars.
Knife.

Method:

1. Mix dry ingredients together thoroughly.
2. Melt the copha in the saucepan over a low heat until it is all melted but not hot.
3. Pour copha over dry ingredients, mix, add vanilla and mix well.
4. Pour the mixture into a shallow oven tray and cool in the refrigerator.
5. When firm, cut into cubes and store in airtight jars.

CANDIED POPCORN***

Ingredients:
½ cup unpopped "popping corn"
2 tablespoons cooking oil
2 cups sugar
1 cup water
½ teaspoon food colouring
(eg. cochineal.)

Equipment:
Large saucepan with lid OR
Electric frypan with glass lid
Bowl
Spoon
Small bowl of cold Water
Large tray

Method:
1. Heat oil in large saucepan until very hot, add corn, cover with lid and shake over heat until the popping sound stops.
2. Remove from heat, place popcorn in bowl to cool.
3. Put sugar, water and food colouring in a large saucepan, stir over a low heat until the sugar dissolves.
4. Bring to the boil, simmer uncovered until, when you drop some of this toffee from a spoon into cold water, the toffee drops set firmly. Now the toffee is ready.
5. Remove from heat, pour popcorn into toffee, stir contantly until toffee thoroughly coats popcorn, remove from pan and spread on a large tray to cool.

Note: With a needle and a long piece of cotton you can make candied popcorn (in several different colours) into a necklace or Christmas tree decorations.

CHRISTMAS SHORTBREADS***

Ingredients:

220g butter (room temperature)
100g castor sugar
280g plain flour
60g cornflour
1 pkt glace cherries
½ teaspoon baking powder
¼ teaspoon salt.
Icing sugar
Food colourings: green red yellow
Coloured cachous.

Equipment:

Bowl
Wooden spoon or Electric mixer
Flour sifter
Floured board
Sharp knife or shape cutters.

Method:

1. Cream butter and sugar by mashing together with a wooden spoon or electric mixer until the mixture is white and creamy.
2. Gradually work in the sifted flour, cornflour, baking powder, salt and cherries. Knead the mixture thoroughly with your hands.
3. Press (do not roll) onto a board, 1 cm thick, and cut out Christmas shapes, using cutters or paper patterns copied from this book.
4. Bake in a moderately slow oven 160°C (325°F) gas for 20 minutes or until pale golden brown.
5. Ice Christmas tree with green icing, decorate with cachous. Ice star yellow, with cachous. Ice Santa with red hat and clothes, piped white beard, eyes and nose, cachou buttons.

EASTER EGGS *

Ingredients:

4 eggs
Outer skins of 4 onions
Water

Equipment:

4 rubber bands.
Large saucepan
Cheesecloth
Spoon
Scissors

Method:

1. Cut four squares of cheesecloth about 25 cm x 25 cm.
2. Place an egg in the centre of each square, and wrap onion skins around each of the eggs and secure with rubber bands.
3. Carefully bring the edges of the squares together, to form a little bag holding the wrapped egg.
4. Wrap this bag tightly around the egg and tie with the string as close as possible to the egg.
5. Place the eggs in the large saucepan and cover with cold water.
6. Bring the water slowly to the boil, boil for four minutes.
7. Pour off hot water, pour on cold water, remove eggs from saucepan and undo the string.
8. When cheescloth and skins are removed the hardboiled eggs have an attractive mottled appearance.

NOTE: Prepared Easter egg dyes can also be bought, or you can try dipping a hardboiled egg into beetroot juice or plum juice.

DRINKS

EGG FLIP* (No Heat)

Ingredients:

1 egg
¾ Cup warm or cold milk
1 teaspoon sugar
4 drops vanilla essence
Nutmeg (if you like)

Equipment:

Bowl
Rotary beater
Teaspoon
Measuring cup
Strainer
Glass

Method:

1. Break egg into basin, add sugar.
2. Beat egg and sugar until frothy.
3. Add milk and vanilla. Stir thoroughly.
4. Pour through strainer into glass and serve. Sprinkle with nutmeg if you like.

SPIDER* (No Heat)

Ingredients:

1 cup lemonade — any flavour
Vanilla or strawberry ice cream
2 ice blocks

Equipment:

Bowl
Rotary beater or fork
Ice cream scoop
Glass

Method:

1. Pour lemonade and ice into the bowl, add a scoop of ice cream.
2. Beat with fork or rotary beater until ice cream is half blended; pour into a glass and serve.
3. Spiders can also be made by shaking lemonade and ice cream in a jar with a lid.

SMOOTHIE * (No Heat)

Ingredients:

One serve of soft fruit, eg. 1 banana, or
6 strawberries or 1 peach
1 cup cold milk
1 cup fruit yoghurt
2 iceblocks
1 tablespoon honey (if you like)

Equipment:

Blender
Measuring cups
Large serving glass

Method:

1. Place all ingredients in the blender, blend until smooth and pour into the glass.

RECIPES WITH
FUNNY NAMES

WELSH RAREBIT**

Ingredients:

1 cup grated tasty cheese
½ teaspoon mustard
1 tablespoon butter (for toast)
1 teaspoon worcester sauce
a dash of pepper
3 tablespoons milk
4 slices hot buttered toast.

Equipment:

toaster
spreading knife
plate
grater
double saucespan
oven mitt.

Not Welsh Rabbit!

Method:

1. Make the toast and butter it. Keep it hot if you can, in a "low" oven.
2. Put grated cheese, milk, mustard, pepper and Worcester sauce in the top of the double saucepan. Put boiling water in the bottom part of the saucepan, fit together and heat gently.
3. When the ingredients are all well blended and mixture is creamy, pour over the toast and serve immediately.

ANGELS ON HORSEBACK*

Ingredients:

oysters or scallops
lemon juice
black pepper
½ rasher of lean bacon (rind
  removed) per oyster.

Equipment:

plate
fry pan, griller or oven
toothpicks.

Method:

1. Sprinkle oysters or scallops with lemon juice and a little pepper.
2. Wrap each oyster in bacon and fasten with a toothpick.
3. Place under hot griller, or in fry pan or oven, cook quickly until bacon is lightly browned. Serve immediately.

DEVILS ON HORSEBACK*

Ingredients:

large prunes
½ rasher of lean bacon (rind
  removed) per prune
1 square of bread per prune.

Equipment:

plate
toothpicks
oven tray.

Method:

1. Remove the stones from the prunes.
2. Roll each prune in a strip of bacon, and fasten with a toothpick.
3. Place on squares of bread and bake for about 20 minutes in a moderate oven 180°C (350°F) gas. Serve hot!

HEDGEHOG* (No Bake)

Ingredients: **Equipment:**

½ cup butter   saucepan
½ cup sugar   spoon
3 tablespoons cocoa   shallow tin
1 egg   rolling pin
250 grams sweet biscuits (e.g. Marie). plastic bag.

Method:
1. Crush the biscuits to small crumbs in a food processor or place in a plastic bag, and roll with a rolling pin.
2. Place butter, sugar and cocoa in saucepan over a low heat. Stir occasionally.
3. When sugar is dissolved, take saucepan off heat and add egg, then crushed biscuits. Mix well.
4. Press the mixture into a shallow tin with the back of a spoon.
5. Cool in the refrigerator, then ice with chocolate icing and cut into squares.
Variation: ¾ cup of mixed fruit and nuts may be added.

TRUFFLES* (No Heat)

Ingredients: **Equipment:**

250 gram malt biscuits   rolling pin
1½ cups coconut   plastic bag
1 tablespoon cocoa   bowl
1 tin condensed milk.   spoon

Method:

1. Crush biscuits finely (see Hedgehog receipe.)
2. Mix with coconut and cocoa. Add condensed milk and mix well.
3. Roll into little balls, toss in coconut or chocolate sprinkles. Chill in refrigerator.

TOAD IN THE HOLE***

Ingredients:
500g thick sausages, boiled.
125g flour
½ teaspoon salt
1 egg
300ml milk
fat for frying; e.g. dripping.

Equipment:
roasting dish
bowl
flour sifter
spoon.

Method:
1. Sift the flour and salt into the bowl and make a well in the centre.
2. Put the egg and half the milk (150 ml) into the well, and start mixing from the centre, gradually working in all the flour from the sides.
3. Add the rest of the milk and beat throroughly to mix in plenty of air.
4. Heat some dripping in the roasting dish. Melted dripping should be at least 2 cm deep.
5. Peel the skins off the boiled sausages and heat them in the dripping for 5 minutes.
6. When dripping is very hot, pour in the batter and cook in a very hot oven 250°C (500°F) gas for about 10 minutes.
7. Reduce the heat to 215°C (425°F) gas for another 30 minutes, or until the batter is cooked. It should be well risen, brown and hollow inside. Remove from fat and serve hot.

GROW YOUR OWN INGREDIENTS

Many fruits and vegetables can be easily grown at home!

FRUIT TREES AND NUT TREES

Save apple seeds, orange pips and apricot stones. Plant them in your garden about 2 cm deep in soft soil, and in a position where they will be watered often. Choose fresh walnuts in their shells, and plant them, shell and all.

It takes a long time but eventually, if kept moist, little apple, orange, apricot or walnut trees may start to grow!

POTATO PLANTS

All potatoes have little marks called "eyes". Sprouts for new plants grow from these eyes.

Take a large, old potato and cut it into quarters. Each quarter must have at least one eye on it.

Plant the four potato pieces in soft soil in your garden, and keep them moist. They will grow into plants which, when the leaves die down, will have lots of new potatoes underground!

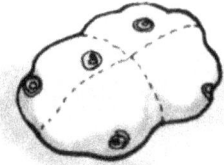

AVOCADO TREES

Save an avocado pit, stick toothpicks partway into it on each side as shown, and place it on top of a milk bottle full of water. Leave it near a window, making sure that the water always touches the bottom of the seed.

After a while roots will grow down, leaves will grow up, and you will have an avocado tree to plant in your garden!

MUSTARD AND CRESS INDOOR GARDENS

Mustard and cress seeds, mixed can be bought in packets from plant nurseries. The shoots grow to about 2 to 3 cm high; that's when they should be cut off and sprinkled on salads or eaten in salad sandwiches, for a peppery taste. All parents enjoy them and most kids do too!

Mustard and cress gardens can be grown on a dinner plate placed near a window. Cover the plate with a layer of cotton wool about 1 cm thick. Wet the cotton wool thoroughly and sprinkle the seeds on, not too thickly.

Keep wetting the cotton wool every day. It should never be allowed to dry out.

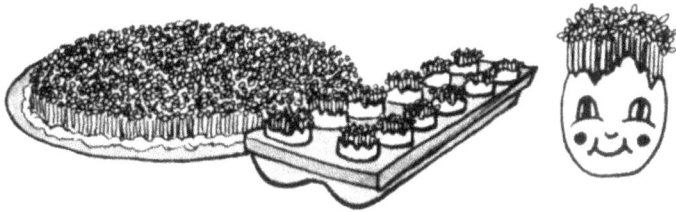

Mustard and cress eggheads can be made by saving eggshells from boiled eggs, and drawing funny faces on them with felt-tip pens. Put the eggshells into an egg carton to keep them upright, and fill with potting soil, then sprinkle with the seeds and keep them moist but not too wet. The green shoots will look like hair!

CRAFTY COOKING

HOME MADE GLUE

Ingredients:

1 cup plain flour
water

Equipment:

bowl
spoon

Method:

Mix flour with enough water to make it gooey and sticky but not runny. This glue goes mouldy after a few weeks but it is fine for papier maché.

PAPIER MACHE MODELLING

Ingredients:

lots of newspaper
bowl of water
lots of home-made glue

Equipment:

A square of old material
  (e.g. old panty-hose).
A central core for your
  model (e.g. cardboard
  toilet rolls or small boxes).

Method:

1 Tear newspaper into lots of tiny pieces, about 2 or 3 cms in diameter
2 Soak the pieces in the bowl of water for several hours (Overnight is best).
3 Pour paper and water through your piece of material or panty-hose to squeeze out the water.
4 Put the soggy paper back into the bowl and gradually add homemade glue until the mixture feels like clay.
5 This mixture can be modelled onto a central core or used to make easy items to start with, such as eggs, small dolls or balls.
6 Allow to dry for several days at room temperature.
7 Paint with bright colours. You can make decorations for your Christmas tree with papier maché!

PLAYDOUGH - COOKED*

Ingredients:

1 cup plain flour
1 cup water
½ cup salt
1 tablespoon cooking oil
2 tablespoons cream of tartar
Few drops food colouring.

Equipment:

Large saucepan
Wooden spoon
Measuring cups and spoons.

Method:

1. Put all the ingredients into the large saucepan.
2. Mix together and cook on a low heat, stirring all the time until the mixture becomes thick. This happens SUDDENLY!
3. Cool, and store in the refrigerator, wrapped tightly in a plastic bag with no holes in it. This playdough keeps indefinitely.

PLAYDOUGH - UNCOOKED*

Ingredients:

2 cups plain flour
1 cup salt
1 tablespoon cooking oil
water
Few drops of food colouring.

Equipment:

Bowl
Measuring cups and spoons
Mixing spoon.

Method:

Mix together flour, salt, colouring and oil, with enough water to make a workable dough. Store in a plastic bag in the refrigerator. This dough will not keep fresh for more than two weeks.

FINGERPAINT RECIPE 1

Ingredients:

2 tablespoons sugar
½ cup cornflour
2 cups cold water
Food colouring.

Equipment:

Saucepan
Mixing spoon
Measuring cups and spoons
3 to 4 containers.

Method:

1. In the saucepan mix flour and sugar together, then add water.
2. Stir over low heat until well blended.
3. Divide mixture into three or four parts and add a different food colour to each.

FINGERPAINT RECIPE 2

This fingerpaint washes easily out of clothes!

Ingredients:

6 tablespoons cornflour
½ cup cold water
¼ cup Lux flakes or other pure
    soap flakes
2 teaspoons food colouring
½ tablespoon Dettol or other
    household antiseptic liquid
boiling water.

Equipment:

Measuring jug
Saucepan
Spoon
Measuring spoons.

Method:

1. Blend cornflour and cold water in measuring jug.
2. Add boiling water until the level of the mixture comes up to 700 ml, pour into saucepan and bring to the boil, stirring constantly — Boil one minute.
3. Remove from heat, add colouring and soap flakes and stir until soap is dissolved. Stir in antiseptic liquid.

INDEX

THE PARENTS' TIME OFF SERIES

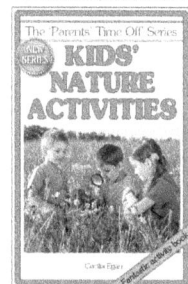

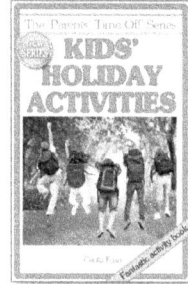

The Parents' Time Off Series

KIDS' MAGICAL ACTIVITIES

The Parents' Time Off Series

KIDS' COOKING ACTIVITIES

The Parents' Time Off Series

KIDS' HANDS-ON CRAFT ACTIVITIES

The Parents' Time Off Series

KIDS' CREATIVE CRAFT ACTIVITIES

The Parents' Time Off Series

KIDS' FUN CRAFT ACTIVITIES

The Parents' Time Off Series

KIDS' GAMES BOOK 1

The Parents' Time Off Series

KIDS' NATURE ACTIVITIES

The Parents' Time Off Series

KIDS' GAMES BOOK 2

The Parents' Time Off Series

KIDS' GARDENING ACTIVITIES

The Parents' Time Off Series

KIDS' HOLIDAY ACTIVITIES

SOME MORE BOOKS IN OUR CHILDRENS' SERIES:

The Parents' Time Off Series:

- Kids' Magical Activities

- Kids' Gardening Activities

- Kids' Cooking Activities

- Kids' Hands-On Craft Activities

- Kids' Fun Craft Activities

- Kids' Creative Craft Activities

- Kids' Games Book 1

- Kids' Games Book 2

- Kids' Nature Activities

- Kids' Holiday Activities

Classic Fairytales from Tolkien's Bookshelf:

- Grimms' Fairytales - Illustrated

- The Red Fairy Book - Illustrated

- The Princess and the Goblin - Illustrated.

- The Story of King Arthur and his Knights - Illustrated

Find out more on our website!

www.leavesofgoldpress.com

Princess Pam
Fell Into the Jam

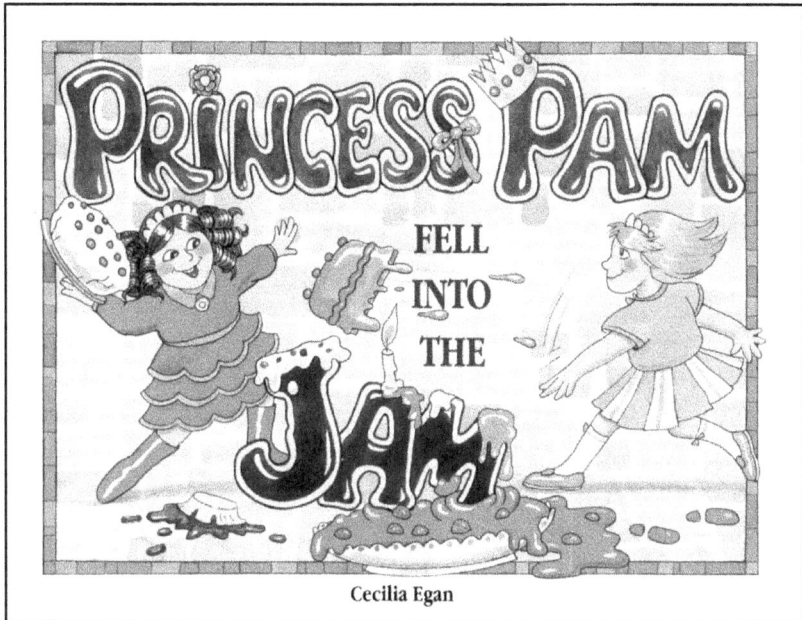

Cecilia Egan

More than a hilarious rhyme, this is a slapstick comedy that causes a riot of laughter when read aloud. Princess Pam and her messy sisters appeal to every child.

The rollicking rhymes, the unconventional story and the lively, detailed pictures combine to make one of the funniest and most original children's books published.

www.ingramcontent.com/pod-product-compliance
Lightning Source LLC
Chambersburg PA
CBHW060553100426
42742CB00013B/2544